JACOB IS MY MAN!

I LOVE RPATTZ

SUNBIRD

Published by Ladybird Books Ltd 2010
A Penguin Company
Penguin Books Ltd, 80 Strand, London, WC2R 0RL, UK
Penguin Books Australia Ltd, Camberwell, Victoria, Australia.
Penguin Group (NZ), 67 Apollo Drive, Rosedale, North Shore.
0632, New Zealand (a division of Pearson New Zealand Ltd)

Sunbird is a trade mark of Ladybird Books Ltd

www.ladybird.com

ISBN: 978-1-40939-027-5
10 9 8 7 6 5 4 3 2
Printed in Italy

Robert, Taylor, Kristen

The Unauthorized Annual 2011

Contents

All About Robert

Taylor Time

Kristen's World

Get The Look!

Quizzes & Fun

Shining Stars

It's official: *Twilight* fever has gripped the world and the young stars of the film series have been launched into the celebrity stratosphere. Yes, Robert Pattinson, Taylor Lautner and Kristen Stewart are seriously hot right now!

Rob is totally dazzling as the brooding, beautiful vampire Edward Cullen, Taylor is seriously smoking as the wild wolf Jacob Black and Kristen is strong and inspiring as our favourite heroine, Bella Swan. It's no surprise that fans all over the globe have been captivated by this talented trio, and their profiles are getting bigger by the day as they rack up movie offers, magazine covers and column inches.

But we're hungry for more! Who is Rob's ideal woman? What makes Taylor tick? And how the heck can we get Kristen's look so we can bag a hottie of our own?

Well, fret no more! Because this book is packed with delicious gossip, gorgeous photos, fab quizzes and hot style-tips. Read on to discover all you've ever wanted to know about your favourite stars and personalize your book with the cool stickers inside . . .

Meet . . . Robert Pattinson

Robert is well on his way to global super-stardom and sets hearts on fire wherever he goes! But who is the man behind the vampire? Find out what really makes him tick . . .

The Basics

Name: Robert Thomas Pattinson
Nicknames: Rob, RPattz, Patty
Birthdate: 13 May, 1986
Star sign: Taurus
Hometown: London, England
Height: 6'1"

The Early Days

Rob was born in Barnes, London and raised by his parents, Clare and Robert. He has two older sisters, who are also very creative – Lizzy is a singer/songwriter and Victoria works in advertising. From an early age, Rob acted in school productions and was always more interested in expressing his creative side than getting good grades! By the time he moved to senior school at age 12, he had discovered hair gel and girls, and had become a bit of a bad-boy rebel (with a heart of gold). He says his school reports were, "always pretty bad – I never, ever did my homework. I always turned up for lessons as I liked my teachers, but my report said I didn't try very hard."

Rising Star

The turning point in Rob's acting career came at age 15, when his dad encouraged him to join his local drama club, the Barnes Theatre Group – but not necessarily for artistic reasons! He says, "I only did it because my dad saw a bunch of pretty girls in a restaurant and he asked them where they came from and they said drama group. He said, 'Son, that is where you need to go.'" While Rob may have joined for fun at first, his talent became obvious pretty quickly, and he was cast as the lead in his second play. Rob says, "It is unbelievable how this stroke of luck has completely changed my entire life . . . I owe everything to that little club." Soon, Rob was spotted by an actors' agent and began auditioning for professional jobs. His first big break came with an appearance in the TV film *Ring of the Nibelungs*, but it would be his role as Cedric Diggory in *Harry Potter and the Goblet of Fire* that really got him noticed.

Rob took his first big acting job very seriously. He totally immersed himself in his role, reading the *Harry Potter* books over and over and scouring the Internet for fan tips on his character – this shows just how dedicated he is to his craft and how much preparation he puts into creating realistic roles. When the film came out, Rob was a little overwhelmed by the crazy attention. He was thrust into the limelight and admits he didn't deal very well with it at first – "I'm not nearly as cocky as I was. I was a real prat for the first month. I didn't talk to anyone." Rob bravely admitted he was becoming a bit full of himself and made sure he checked his behaviour from then on. What a sweetheart! It was a lesson well-learnt, as the success of the *Potter* films would prepare him for the biggest break of his life – *The Twilight Saga*.

Getting the Job

Rob didn't have the role of Edward Cullen in the bag from the start – neither Stephenie Meyer, nor the director, Catherine Hardwicke, were convinced by his photo! The turning point came in his audition. Rob flew out to meet Catherine in the US and had to rehearse the passionate bedroom kissing scene with Kristen – having never met her before. Rob was very nervous, but his chemistry with Kristen was instant and it was obvious he had to play the part, as Catherine explained, "It was electric. The room shorted out, the sky opened up, and I was like, 'This is going to be good.'" Phew! And what sealed the deal? Kristen Stewart told Catherine, "It has to be Rob."

"He's pretty much one of the most eligible bachelors out there right now."
Ashley Greene (Alice Cullen) on Robert

Robert & *Twilight*

Becoming Edward

Rob's approach to creating the role of Edward Cullen was devoted and painstaking. Two months before filming, he went to Oregon alone and pored over the *Twilight* books. He wanted to truly understand Edward's sense of isolation, so he distanced himself from everybody and started writing a journal in the voice of his character, to really try to think and be like Edward. "I was really concentrating on this job," he says. "I just didn't talk to anybody for ages during the beginning of the shoot. I never went out." Rob began to see the complex nature of the character, a century-old vampire who falls in love with a human girl, but also lusts after her blood. His situation is dark and tragic, and he feels constant passion and danger when he's with her. Rob explains, "He's a conflicted and reluctant vampire. He's a poet, and very deep and profound. He's just extraordinarily troubled." Rob must have found it useful to draw on his own creative personality, something fellow *Twilight* vampire Kellan Lutz noticed straight away – "Rob is definitely Edward. He's so complicated, so poetic . . ." Robert rose to the huge challenge with determination and drive, and his portrayal of Edward is brilliant and sensitive – Stephenie Meyer even said it was "Oscar-worthy". Yes, fans of the books have totally accepted him as the perfect Edward and now follow him wherever he goes!

> "You're not just any famous person. Edward Cullen is such an icon. When you see people on the street, it's not just that they feel like they know you. It's like they need you."
>
> Kristen Stewart on Rob's role

New Moon, Breaking Dawn and *Eclipse*

Robert has grown with his character and was excited to develop Edward's role throughout the other three books. While his part in *New Moon* was smaller, he has always said, "It's the one I connected to the most, and the one that humanized Edward for me the most, as well." The heat really picked up in *Eclipse*, which delved deeper into the love triangle between Edward, Jacob and Bella, in the midst of a huge battle involving the werewolves and vampires. Robert really enjoyed exploring the character's dynamics more deeply, explaining, "All the conflict is really escalated, there's a lot more tension, it's more faster paced". The hype just keeps getting bigger with every movie, and with *Breaking Dawn* already in production in Portland, Oregon, it won't be long before fans get their next Rob fix!

Beyond *Twilight*

Want more Rob? The good news is, he's expanding his repertoire with lots of other film projects! Catch him in *Remember Me, Unbound Captives* and, soon, *Bel Ami* and *Water for Elephants*.

"I go to different cities in the world for screaming sessions."

RPattz on his job

Robert On . . .

Does Rob Pattinson think he's gorgeous? Is he constantly dating? You'll be surprised by the truth!

Girls

So, we all know we love Rob, but what does he look for in a girl? Well, despite feeling shy and a little insecure, he says he's drawn to strong women – though they can be difficult! "Even though it sounds odd, I like self-confidence . . . I mostly like strong girls, but with them, I have the most problems," he admits. Rob also confesses a weakness for kooky ladies with a wild streak – "I'm always shocked by the people who I'm attracted to . . . I generally like people who are a bit crazy." And if you ever meet Rob, how should you play it? Hard to get! It seems he likes the thrill of the chase, as he admits to finding girls very attractive, "when they hate me from the beginning"! There is hope for all you single ladies out there: Rob is a real romantic and believes in soulmates – he just hasn't found the right girl yet . . .

His Looks

With his smouldering eyes, chiselled cheekbones and mussed-up bad-boy hair, Rob sends hearts aflutter all over the globe. In 2009, he was named 'Most Handsome Man in the World' by *Vanity Fair*, and 'Sexiest Man Alive' by *People* magazine. We all know Rob is totally hot – but what makes him even hotter? He's modest, and even embarrassed by his good looks! He says he finds it scary being cast as super-gorgeous characters like the "absurdly handsome" Cedric Diggory, and the "inhumanly beautiful" Edward Cullen, as he doesn't feel like a heart-throb at all. When he auditioned for *Twilight*, he says, "I just thought even having the gall to go in means you're . . . arrogant." In fact, Rob says he has one leg longer than the other, which he thinks makes him look "like an idiot" and he feels more like a "cartoon character" than a movie star. Er, millions of girls disagree with you, Rob!

Co-star Comments

Find out why Rob's fellow actors adore him!

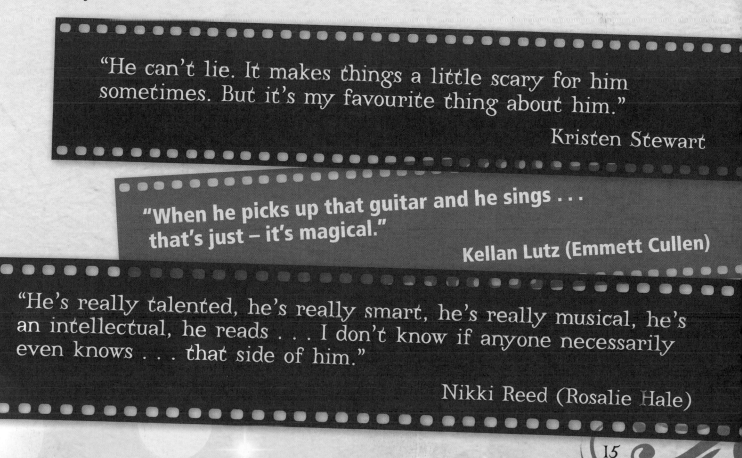

"He can't lie. It makes things a little scary for him sometimes. But it's my favourite thing about him."

Kristen Stewart

"When he picks up that guitar and he sings . . . that's just – it's magical."

Kellan Lutz (Emmett Cullen)

"He's really talented, he's really smart, he's really musical, he's an intellectual, he reads . . . I don't know if anyone necessarily even knows . . . that side of him."

Nikki Reed (Rosalie Hale)

The A–Z of Robert Pattinson

His loves, idols, favourite things and more!

 is for AMERICA

Rob is inspired by our buddies across the pond. He says, "All of my favourite actors are American and I also grew up watching US movies."

 is for BAD GIRLS

The name of Rob's old band.

 is for CLAUDIA

When he was little, his sisters dressed him up as a girl and called him 'Claudia'!

 is for DIET COKE

Rob can't get enough of the sweet stuff.

 is for EXORCIST

This scary movie is Rob's favourite!

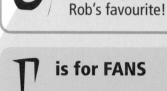 **is for FANS**

Twihards mob the actor wherever he goes and he says it can get quite frightening – "It's kind of like being in some medieval battle!"

 is for GIRLS

Rob has said he can't get a date, because he can't go out. Um, we're free!

 **H is for HAIR**

He once said he never washed it. Ew!

is for INTERNET

Our guy can't help checking out the gossip blogs and fan sites – "It's like reading people's minds, like when you meet someone and you really want to know what they think of you."

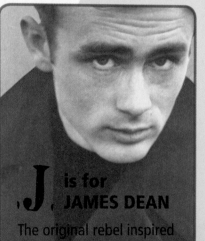

J is for JAMES DEAN

The original rebel inspired Rob's portrayal of Edward Cullen – and his off-camera fashion sense!

k is for KISSING

He loves it – "I always get carried away when I'm kissing. I just go nuts." Swoon!

L is for LONDON

RPattz adores his hometown and gets upset when he's away too long.

M is for MODEL

Rob modelled from age 12–16 and admits, "I was such a terrible model. I was really tall but still looked like a six-year-old."

n. is for NEW MOON

This is Rob's favourite book in the *Twilight* series.

O is for THE OFFICE

RPattz thinks the UK TV show is the best!

P is for PATTY

The name of Rob's terrier. He adores his dog and hates leaving him in the UK.

Q is for QUEEN'S ENGLISH

The actor's English accent has American girls swooning over him!

S is for SONGWRITER

Rob loves composing music, although he's said he is too scared to release anything at the moment.

t is for TRUE ROMANCE

"I've always had a thing for Patricia Arquette. She was my childhood pin-up. I liked her in *True Romance*. I watched that about 15 years ago and she kind of struck a chord with me."

r is for RAY-BANS

Rob always looks totally hot in his trademark shades.

u is for UGG BOOTS

Want to bag Robert? Don't wear these cosy boots – they put him off!

U is for WORKING OUT

Going shirtless in *New Moon* was "very nerve-wracking," he says. And seeing Taylor on set made it worse! "It's like, 'Jeez, now I have to go to the gym.'"

V is for VAN MORRISON

This soulful singer is Rob's fave musician. He says the song 'Wild Night' always makes him happy.

X is for X-FACTOR

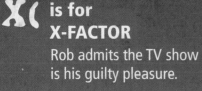

Rob admits the TV show is his guilty pleasure.

y is for YOUTUBE

The actor's favourite website.

Z is for ZZZZs!

Robert once missed an entire day of filming because he slept through the day! His co-stars say he's always late.

Meet . . . Taylor Lautner

Taylor is officially Hollywood hot property! With an obsessive army of
Team Jacob fans, he makes girls swoon at the sheer sight of his abs.
But there's more to Tay than a buff body; discover how the
determined young idol had to fight for success
every step of the way . . .

The Basics

Name: Taylor Daniel Lautner
Nicknames: Tay, TLaut
Birthdate: 11 February, 1992
Star sign: Aquarius
Hometown: Michigan, USA
Height: 5'10½"

Grrrrr!

All grown up

Karate Kid

Taylor grew up in Grand Rapids, Michigan, with his mum, Deborah, dad, Dan and younger
sister, Makena. He's got a mixed heritage – French, Dutch, German and, like Jacob, Native
American (Ottawa and Potawatomi to be specific!). Taylor was a straight-A student at school,
but his main love was sport – "I did wrestling, football, baseball, martial arts and before
long, I was forced to narrow things down, because you just can't do everything." He decided
to focus on karate and, when he channelled his energy, it paid off – he was world number
one by age 12! At such a young age, Taylor was already showing his natural drive,
enthusiasm and dedication – something that would pay off as he launched himself into the
difficult world of acting . . .

Showbiz Calling

It was Taylor's karate teacher, Mike Chat, who first suggested he go into show business.
Mike had connections and started putting Tay up for auditions in Hollywood. Taylor caught
the acting bug and was soon travelling to LA once a month for auditions. Although he
wasn't landing any parts, he only became more disciplined and dedicated to his goal, as he

"Jacob's character becomes very cool and has a lot more depth
in the rest of the series. I'm definitely Team Jacob."

Taylor picks his team!

explained, "From karate, I had the confidence and drive to push myself." When his parents realized how focused and resolved he was, they decided to take a chance on his future and moved to Los Angeles so he could pursue his dream full-time.

Making his Mark

Once in California, Taylor signed up with an actors' agent and started hitting the audition circuit big time. Success didn't come easily though and he had to face many rejections at the beginning, but he says this experience only spurred him on further – "You can't just get down and quit because it's very, very difficult." Taylor knew acting was tough and competitive, and that it could take years of hard work before a big pay-off, but his strength and determination helped him persevere. He took extra acting and voice classes and, slowly but surely, he started winning roles on US TV shows like *The Bernie Mac Show* and *The Nick & Jessica Variety Hour*, as well as voiceover work on cartoons. He built his CV steadily, until he was rightly rewarded with his first big break, age 13, landing the lead role of Sharkboy in *The Adventures of Sharkboy and Lavagirl 3-D*. He received plenty of good reviews for his sincere, natural performance and within months had lined up his next role, in *Cheaper by the Dozen 2*. Taylor had tasted success and as November 2007 rolled around, he received a call that would thrust him firmly into the spotlight . . .

Taylor & Twilight

Twilight Journey

When Taylor first found out he had an audition for *Twilight*, he'd never read the books and wasn't sure what the big deal was. That soon changed! After reading for the director, he looked up *Twilight* on the Internet and got a huge surprise. "I realized how big it was . . . I started hearing about all the hype, all the fans. I thought, 'Oh my goodness. If I get this, it'll be huge.' I realized I really want this." He had an agonizing month-long wait, then got the news he'd been waiting for – he'd landed the role of Jacob Black!

"I'm having the time of my life." Taylor on filming *The Twilight Saga*

Becoming Jacob

Taylor immediately read Stephenie Meyer's books and got hooked. He felt an instant connection to his new part – "He's really friendly and outgoing and just talkative and easy to relate to. That's totally me." Taylor also felt it was important to understand Jacob's Native American heritage; he studied the myths and legends of the Quileute tribe and even went to meet ten tribal members. "They're always helping each other," he says. "They're always there for each other. So I just want to make sure I can bring that part of Jacob alive." Although his role in *Twilight* was small, the fans embraced him as their beloved Jacob. Taylor couldn't wait for *New Moon*, but there was a problem: would he be given the part?

Proving Himself

When the film company confirmed that *New Moon* would go ahead, Taylor's future was in doubt; there were concerns that he couldn't undergo the massive physical transformation required for the role. Well, good thing for us that Taylor loves a challenge! With typical steely determination, he devoted himself to the cause – "As soon as I stopped filming *Twilight*, I got back home, hit the gym and worked very, very hard." He started a high-protein diet, worked out seven days a week with a personal trainer, and put on 30 pounds of sheer muscle! It did the trick and Taylor won his role back.

New Moon Rising

Taylor was delighted to be back in the cast and threw himself into developing the more complex character that Jacob reveals in the sequels. He was especially fascinated by the conflicting sides of Jake's personality – "His Native American side is very friendly and outgoing. He loves Bella and is very loyal to Bella and his dad. But on the werewolf side, he's fierce and attacking, with a huge temper." The other key focus for Taylor was Jacob's blossoming relationship with Bella Swan – a friendship that deepens into love: "Jacob brings Bella out of this huge depression . . . Jacob is her sun. He brings her alive." The emotional scenes with Kristen Stewart stretched him as an actor, and were his favourite moments of filming – "The pivotal scenes in the movie, like Jacob's break-up scene." And his other favourite scenes? The stunts, which he performed himself! Totally hot.

Eclipse and Breaking Dawn

Taylor loved shooting his favourite book, *Eclipse*, because of the fast-paced action and intense emotion. "I just love that it's the height of the love triangle because Edward, Jacob and Bella are physically together," he says. So who does he think she should have chosen? "I personally love Jacob and Bella's relationship," he admits, "and how they began as friends. They are so much more open, and can tell each other anything. And Bella and Edward's relationship, it's always tense. It's always serious." Well, Bella made her choice, but never fear, we've got even more Jake to look forward to in *Breaking Dawn*!

Beyond Twilight

Want even more Tay? Check him out in *Valentine's Day*, and coming up, we get to see him in super-strecthy super-hero mode in *Stretch Armstong*!

21

Taylor Tidbits

What does Taylor look for in a girl? What do his co-stars
really think of him? Check out our Tay trivia!

Tay and Romance

With his smokin' brown eyes, body to die for and gorgeous, glittering smile, it's no surprise
that Taylor is a bit of a ladies' man! He's been linked with plenty of pretty young starlets,
including Miley Cyrus, Selena Gomez and Taylor Swift. The good news is, he's just as likely
to go out with a normal girl as a super-famous actress – as he says, "I don't exclude anyone."
Yessss! So, do you fit the bill? Well, Taylor loves a girl who can be herself: "Somebody who
can just open up and be free and not try to be somebody different," and he likes to have a
laugh with his lady, "Be a dork, have fun, don't be all uptight!" And if you do get a
one-on-one with Tay, do not play it cool! "Playing hard to get is not the way to
win me over. I'm definitely more for the girl who can smile and laugh all the time
and just have a good time!" And finally, the quality he most likes in a girl? "Loyalty".
Um, like you'd cheat with that on your arm.

Co-star Comments

"He's one of the most steady, good guys I've met."   Kristen Stewart

"That is someone who really respected what he was doing and brought an
honesty and integrity and an innocence and a warmth to a character that
was somewhat intimidating to play."   Nikki Reed

"He's extremely charismatic. And he had his work cut out for him,
because at first, everyone was crazed over Edward."   Ashley Greene

"I saw him and thought, ' . . . I'm going to get fired.'"   RPattz on seeing Tay's abs

Taylor's Awards:

No 1 on *Access Hollywood*'s 'Top 5 Hollywood Abs' list
One of *People* magazine's '100 Most Beautiful People', 2009
Teen Choice Awards – 'Fresh Face Male', 2009

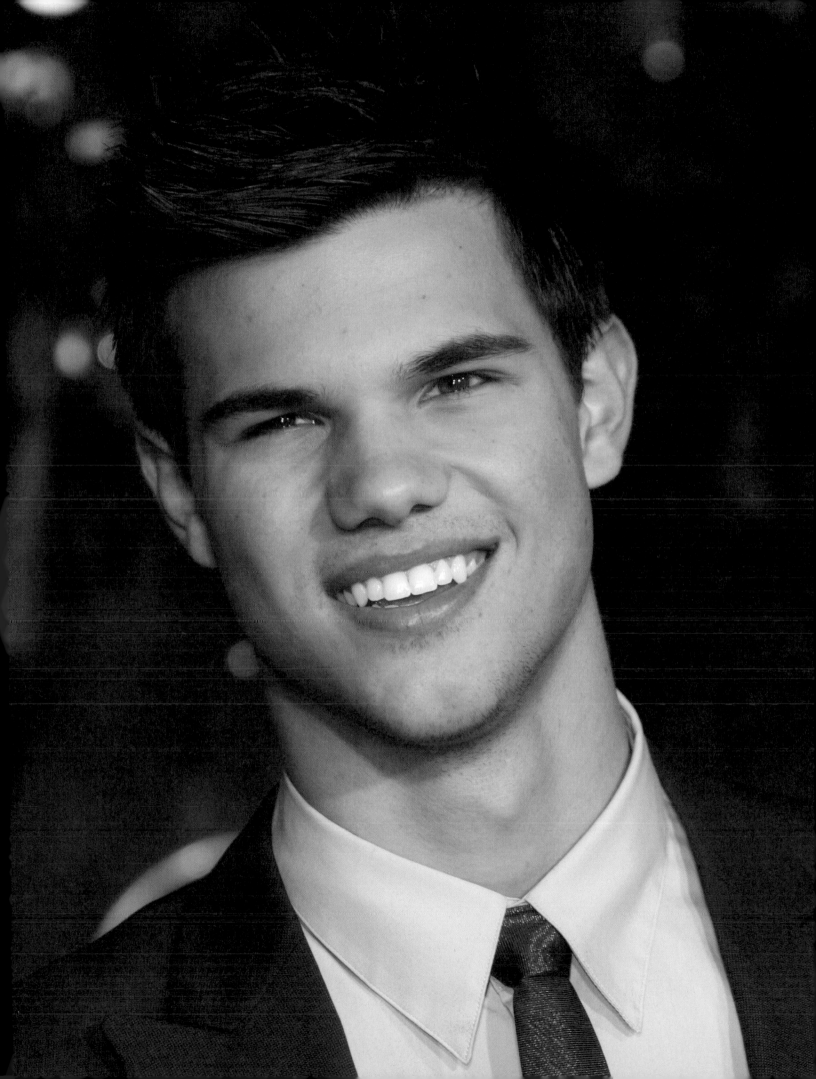

The A-Z of Taylor Lautner

 is for AMERICAN IDOL

Taylor loves the US talent show.

B is for BEST SMILE

When he was at school, Taylor won a prize for 'Best Smile'! US TV host Tyra Banks also said he has "The best teeth I've seen on my show since 50 Cent was on." Go, Tay!

 **is for CHINESE FOOD**

Taylor's takeaway of choice.

d is for DARK KNIGHT

Along with *Iron Man*, this is his favourite film.

e is for ECLIPSE

Taylor likes this book the best, because, "The constant tension going on between Jacob and Edward is hilarious and Bella's being drawn between the two guys."

F is for FERRARI ENZO

This mean machine is Tay's dream car.

f is for GYM

Taylor put in serious work to get those abs – but he's embarrassed of showing his body off! "It's actually quite uncomfortable knowing so many people are seeing that!"

H is for HIP-HOP

He used to break-dance with the group 'LA Hip Kids'.

i is for ICE CREAM

Taylor craves his favourite flavour, 'cake batter'. Sounds weird.

J is for JASON BOURNE

Tay totally loves Matt Damon in the 'Bourne' series.

 is for KLEIN (CALVIN, THAT IS!)

Taylor's been spotted in the designer underwear!

L is for LEATHER JACKET

Tay loves a bit of biker chic.

M is for MEGAN FOX

His celebrity crush! We'll try not to be intimidated . . .

N is for NAILS
Naughty Taylor bites his.

P is for PLAYSTATION
Taylor chills out by playing sports games on his console.

Q is for QUIRK
"One of my worst habits is that I have Restless Legs Syndrome. I can never stop bouncing my knee."

S is for SPIDERS
His biggest fear!

V is for VANS
Taylor loves these cool skate shoes.

W is for WOLVERINES
The Michigan American football team he supports. How fitting!

X is for XTREME MARTIAL ARTS
Taylor has been doing this special form of karate since he was six! He's a black belt and has won multiple world champion titles. We're feeling a little faint.

Z is for ZOOMS
Taylor has been spotted in these fresh Nike basketball shoes.

O is for OMJ!
The Jacob fans are just as passionate as the Edward brigade and while Taylor says it can get scary, he loves his team! "We're definitely thankful to have them behind us. That's our driving force."

R is for ROXY
Taylor's super-cute Maltese terrier.

T is for TWITTER
Beware, fans! Taylor says he doesn't have an account, although plenty of people pretend to be him!

U is for UP

Y is for YUMMY!
Um, need we say more?

Are you Team Edward or Team Jacob?

Find out which *Twilight* guy is your perfect love match by following the chart below.

You get a little scared and excited every time you see your crush. — **YES** → You love old-fashioned romance.

You love old-fashioned romance.
- **YES** ↓
- **NO** →

You get a little scared and excited every time you see your crush.
- **NO** ↓

You fall in love easily.
- **YES** ↓
- **NO** →

You like to feel a little bit dangerous around your guy.
- **YES** →
- **NO** ↓

When you're in a relationship, nothing else matters.
- **YES** ↓
- **NO** →

You prefer guys who are deep and intense.
- **NO**
- **YES** ↓

You hate it when your guy is too secretive.
- **NO** ↓
- **YES** →

You need a guy to be totally open and honest, all the time.
- **YES** ↓

When you fall in love, it's forever. You only get one true love.
- **YES** ↓

- **NO**
- **NO** ↓

Your man is elegant and cool.
- **YES** ↓

You like to spend every possible minute with your crush.
- **NO**
- **YES** ↓

Team Edward!

Your dream guy is Mr Cullen. You are both true romantics and when you fall in love, you do it wholeheartedly! You like a guy to be intense, passionate and deeply devoted. You don't mind that Edward can be aloof and mysterious sometimes, because you know he'd do anything for you. You like his old-fashioned ideas of romance and believe a guy should protect and care for his girl.

26

START HERE!

YES ← | **NO** →
You like guys who are very mysterious.

NO ↓

You think friendship is more important than passion in a relationship.

You love guys who are playful and fun.

YES ↓

You like a guy who is comforting above all else.

NO

You love a guy with a really buff body.

NO ↓ — **YES** ↓

You love laughing with a boyfriend.

NO

You adore being cuddled.

YES ↓

You like guys who are light-hearted and funny.

Your guy has to be very mature.

NO — **YES** ↓

YES — **NO** ↓

You love reading and learning.

A party is your idea of the perfect date

NO

YES ↓

You don't mind if your guy isn't perfect.

NO ←

Your boy sometimes loses his temper and you don't mind.

NO ↓ — **YES** ↓

YES ↓

Your guy is fiery and full of life.

NO

YES

Team Jacob!

Your dream guy is Mr Black. You are both warm, playful and open,
and you like love to be a natural, organic process – why rush it?
You like a guy to be fun, adventurous and a little wild. You appreciate
that Jacob is committed, but not too intense – a best mate as well as
a boyfriend. You love his modern attitude; he knows you're strong
and independent and he respects your space.

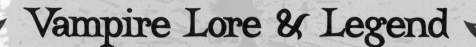

Vampire Lore & Legend

So, you love Robert Pattinson as Edward Cullen?
That's no surprise – vampires have been dazzling people
for years! Discover the history behind the modern legend . . .

Myth and Folklore

Myths about vampires have existed for centuries, all over the world, in many different forms. In ancient culture, people believed in Lilith, a demon who drained men's lives with a single kiss. In the Middle Ages, vamps were corpses who rose from the dead and in the 19th century, writers like Bram Stoker cast them as cool aristos with slick hair and long capes. Although they were all different, these vampires shared things in common: they all thirsted for human blood, had strange powers and strengths, and were more animal than human, with no sense of right and wrong.

Beauty & the Beast

Back in the day, vampires were more dreadful than dazzling. In eastern European folklore, they were short, fat and ugly, with pointed ears, sharp teeth and stinky breath – ew! Victorian writers transformed them into smooth, rich gents with flowing hair, pale skin and expensive clothes. Although they were a little prettier, these vamps still had long dark fingernails, creepy smiles and huge white fangs. Bit of a giveaway. Next, came the vampire of the 20th century horror movie, who was much more charming. With a thick accent, long black cape and coiffed hair, he began to seem really quite appealing, although it wasn't until *Twilight* that vampires became truly beautiful.

Becoming Undead

In old myths, vampires were not created with a bite, but were destined by birth or death to walk with the undead. Babies could be cursed in the womb; if a pregnant mother saw a black cat, ate too much salt or was looked at by a witch, she might be in for a nasty surprise. In death, sinners like murderers, thieves and other criminals had to watch out – they were most likely to become vampires after being buried. In recent legend, vampire creation hinges on the bite. Once the victim is bitten on the neck, they waste away until they die and are then reborn as a vampire.

The *Twilight* Vampires

In the *Twilight* series, Stephenie Meyer has created an entirely unique breed of vampire. They are stronger, cleverer and more stunningly beautiful than any other vampire and have very few weaknesses. They are not harmed by garlic, holy water or sunlight – although they use these old stories to help hide their true identity. Some of the Twivamps, like Edward, Alice and Aro, also possess extra-special abilities. But most importantly, the Cullens have a strong sense of moral choice and possess a conscience; they are more like humans than any other vampires before them.

"Love can be
more lethal than a
vampire bite."

Robert Pattinson

"Vampires are
just cool."

Ashley Greene

Werewolf Lore & Legend

Myth & Folklore

The earliest werewolf story comes from Greek mythology – legend has it that a king called Lycaon served up some human flesh at a party and the god Zeus punished him by turning him into a wolf. Werewolf tales became popular in ancient Rome, too, then spread all through Europe like wildfire. In these old stories, werewolves were mostly downright evil fellas who were transformed into wolves by the Devil and attacked humans. Over in the US, many Native American tribes also have their own werewolf legends and Stephenie Meyer used the Quileute stories to create her *Twilight* pack.

Quileute Legend

Let's get technical. As Edward explains in *Breaking Dawn*, the Quileutes aren't true werewolves, they're shape-shifters, because they have the power to choose when they transform. According to real-life Quileute legend, a wandering sorcerer called Q'Wati travelled to their land and couldn't find any humans, so he transformed two wolves into people: the first members of the tribe. Even the tribal name 'Quileute' comes from their word for wolf, 'Kwoli'. Stephenie Meyer used this myth as a base for her story in the *Twilight* series, but developed it in her own way. In her version, the Quileutes have kept the ability to transform back and forth from human to wolf and this is passed down through generations. She also created the myth of the 'Cold Ones', or vampires, for her books.

Werewolf Looks

Werewolves are said to have a telltale appearance: a monobrow; long, curved fingernails; low, drooping ears; hairy palms and a slouchy walk. Gross. And pretty far removed from Jake, with his decidedly hot body.

Grow some Claws

In traditional myths, there are quite a few ways to turn into a werewolf. You might already be one if you were born under a full moon. You could remove all your clothes and pop on a wolfskin belt. Or why not drink rainwater from a wolf's footprint? Failing that, get a group together and sleep outside on a Wednesday or Friday with the moon shining directly on your face. On second thought, don't try these at home. You'll probably catch a cold. Or get arrested.

Twilight Wolves

The Quileute shape-shifters are pretty different to their mythical cousins and Stephenie Meyer gives them some amazing qualities. In human form, they run a very hot body temperature, have the quickest puberty known to man and, um, really nice chests. As wolves, they are huge, strong and very fast – faster than vampires, in fact. They can read each other's thoughts, heal super quickly and 'phase' at will (not just on a full moon). Jacob is a supreme wolf – he has the gene from both sides of his family, and is able to phase more easily than any of the pack, even in mid-air. Most importantly, the Quileute wolves do not hunt humans, but seek to protect them from their sworn enemy – vampires.

"They are sexy in different ways.
But I'll say werewolf. I have to be true to the pack."

Taylor on whether vampires or werewolves are sexier.

Vampire or Werewolf?

Do you run with vampires? Or are you with the wolf pack?
Circle A or B under each question and find out!

1. **What do you like to do in your spare time?**
   a) You love hanging out with your mates.
   b) You like spending time with your boyfriend.

2. **If someone was insulting your friends at school, what would you do?**
   a) Calmly reason with them and ask them to stop.
   b) Immediately fight back – how dare they?

3. **How would you behave on a first date?**
   a) You like to be intense and romantic – discussing life, love and the universe.
   b) You'd prefer to keep it light and sweet – holding hands, smiling and making jokes.

4. **Your favourite type of movie is . . .**
   a) Comedy
   b) Romance

5. **Which words best describe you?**
   a) Passionate, playful, happy.
   b) Secretive, thoughtful, clever.

6. **You have discovered something that a friend should know – but it might hurt them. Do you tell?**
   a) No. It's not worth it if it ruins their happiness.
   b) Definitely. You hate keeping secrets from your mates.

7. **To you, the moon is . . .**
   a) Beautiful
   b) Powerful

8. **What is your worst quality?**
   a) You get upset easily and tend to overreact.
   b) You bottle things up too much and can seem detached.

9. **What is your best quality?**
   a) You are very loving and loyal to your friends.
   b) You keep a calm head in difficult situations.

10. **Do you lose your temper easily?**
    a) No
    b) Yes

11. **What is your idea of a perfect holiday?**
    a) Travelling the world with total freedom.
    b) A remote cottage in a forest with your guy.

12. **You're making a complaint in a shop. How do you go about it?**
    a) Charm the pants off the sales person – you can get what you want with a smile.
    b) Get pretty angry and raise your voice to make sure you get heard.

13. **People often say your skin is:**
    a) A bit warm.
    b) A bit cold.

14. **What type of guy do you fall for?**
    a) Serious, protective and devoted.
    b) Caring, kind and funny.

15. **Who would you rather live with?**
    a) The Quileutes.
    b) The Cullens.

15–22 points
You're a Vampire!

You're mysterious, private and alluring.
Many people are attracted to your looks and
charm, although you don't let just anyone
get close to you – when you do fall in love,
it's deep, passionate and devoted. You don't
let your emotions bubble over and always
seem cool and collected – although deep down,
you're secretly struggling with inner demons!
The Cullens would welcome you with
open arms.

23–30 points
You're a Werewolf!

You're warm, passionate, and caring.
You are naturally playful, fun and chatty
and everyone wants to be your friend –
rightly so, because you're very loyal. You
love to flirt and don't like to get too
intense with guys, too early. People admire
how headstrong and outspoken you are,
although you do have a fiery temper and
don't like to be messed with! You'd fit right
in with the pack at La Push.

"It's a fact
that Edward would
win over Jacob."

Robert Pattinson sides
with the vampires

"Jacob's hot!"

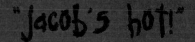

Taylor on his werewolf
character

WOLF GIRL
Style Guide

Day

Nature-loving wolf girls keep it fresh and natural by day. Choose denim, chunky knits, long scarves and wooden jewellery in earthy greens and browns. Layering is key to keeping warm in La Push!

Night

Wolf girls go wild after dark! Express your animal passion with faux fur and shimmering fabrics in rich gold and bronze tones. Grrrr!

TWILIGHTER
Nikki, 20

VAMPIRE GIRL
Style Guide

Get the Look!

Day

Vampire girls are pretty-doll perfect by day. Look for neat skirts, vintage blouses, cute heels and pearls. Think creams, blues and purples. Très chic!

Night

Night-time is playtime for vamps!
Unleash your Volturi dark side with
gothic-inspired lace, velvet, studs
and silk – all in black. Dazzling!

TWILIGHTER
Karen, 19

Twilight Toes

Just grab a plain pair of trainers, sketch your designs on to them with some chalk, then complete with fabric markers or paints. Whose team are you on?

Kristen loves baseball boots!

What you will need:

- A pair of old or new plain trainers
- A piece of chalk
- Some sheets of paper
- Fabric markers or paints

Extras:

- Fake fur
- Coloured ribbon
- Scissors
- Strong glue

Cullen Creepers

Capture the vamp vibe with some lightning bolts, quotes from the books, or even a set of fangs!

Match your paints to the Cullen colour palette: red, black, purple and blue.

Write 'Team Edward' or 'Mrs Cullen' on your shoes – you need to let potential-future-vampire-boyfriends know which side you're on!

Dip the ends of the laces in some red paint to look like blood.

Hot tip:

Make sure you practise your designs on paper before you get stuck in to your trainers!

Get the Look!

Ever been stuck for footwear at a vampire baseball match? Looking for some stylish shoes to help you snag that 'slightly older' boyfriend? Complete your vampire- or wolf-girl look with some customized baseball boots!

Think Jacob: a full moon, a forest or some leaves, a broken heart, paw prints or maybe some scratch marks. Wild!

For a real style statement, glue some fake fur onto your trainers!

Shape-shifting Shoe

Remember to keep the colours earthy: muted browns, black and greens are perfect.

If you're with the pack, write 'Team Jacob' on the side of your shoes. Or – say it loud – 'Vampires Suck'.

Bella's Boots

Can't decide whose team you're on? If you're stuck in the middle like Bella, check out these boots!

true
love
never
dies

Show your devotion to both boys with a drawing of Bella's bracelet, complete with Edward's crystal heart and Jacob's wolf charm.

Bella may be sweet, but she lives on the edge! Add a hint of danger by swapping your laces for red ribbons.

Meet. . . Kristen Stewart

Super pretty, hypercool and Edward Cullen's GFF – Kristen is the envy of girls everywhere! How does she do it? We've got the lowdown on the kooky starlet . . .

The Basics

Name: Kristen Jaymes Stewart
Nicknames: KStew, Kris
Birthdate: 9 April 1990
Star sign: Aries
Hometown: Los Angeles, USA
Height: 5'6"

Kristen Stewart was born and bred in sunny Los Angeles, California, with her three brothers Cameron, Dana and Taylor. Luckily for her, she was surrounded by show business as a child: her dad, John, is a TV stage manager and producer, and her mum, Jules, is a movie script supervisor. Unlike Rob, Kristen knew from an early age that she wanted to act, saying, "It was the first thing I ever thrived at." Her parents weren't so keen, knowing how tough the industry can be for young people, but it didn't take long for fate to come calling . . .

Living the Dream

Kristen was spotted by an actors' agent when she was just eight years old, performing in her school's Christmas play! She started working the audition circuit and picked up mainly non-speaking parts, until age 11, when she was cast in the role that proved to be her first big break — as Jodie Foster's daughter in *Panic Room*. Despite being so young, and working with such a great actress, Kristen held her own and delivered an impressive performance, leading many people to compare her to a young Foster — now that's praise! Kristen herself learned a lot from her mentor: "Watching Jodie shaped my ideas about the way an actor should behave on the set. She's very professional. She's there to do the job."

"You don't need to give reasons for the things you do - you just have to do what you want."

Kristen's view on life

Indie Style

Kristen kept adding to her CV, and at 13, took the starring role in the emotional drama *Speak*, in which she played a complex, withdrawn high school student who suffers a terrible tragedy. At such a young age, she was already impressing critics, who noted her sensitive and realistic portrayal of the character. Kristen was taking her acting career very seriously and after this role, she left school to pursue it full time (don't get any ideas — she still had to be home-schooled on film sets!). In 2006, things picked up at lightning pace, and KStew was in ten films in two years! Most of these were interesting, off-the-wall indie projects, including Sean Penn's *Into the Wild*, in which she played free-spirited hippy Tracy, and first showcased her guitar-playing and singing skills. Kristen was carving a name for herself as a unique young talent — definitely not your typical girly starlet. She was emerging as an outspoken, independent tomboy who knew her own mind. As she says, "I like being in movies that have a great story. I'm not so interested in being a Hollywood star." Kristen thought she'd made a similar decision when she accepted a role in a little vampire flick in November 2007 . . . but she couldn't have been more wrong! That little film was *Twilight*, and it catapulted her to worldwide fame.

Kristen & Twilight

Landing the Part

Kristen was one of the first actors to be cast in *Twilight*. Director Catherine Hardwicke had loved Kristen's mature performance in *Into the Wild*, so went to spend the day with her, shooting scenes on a video camera. When she watched the footage back, the decision was made – "I looked at it and thought, 'Yeah, she's gonna be Bella.'"

Becoming Bella

Kristen realized early on how fiercely the fans love Bella, and that she was under intense pressure to get the part absolutely right. Luckily, she understood what makes Bella so special: "She's awesome and she doesn't know it. She's an odd mix of things . . . a very strong sense of self, but entirely awkward and self-deprecating at the same time. She follows her heart." The result was a beautiful, sensitive portrayal of the different sides of Bella's personality and the fans welcomed her with open arms.

The intense, passionate chemistry between Bella Swan and Edward Cullen is the central focus of the *Twilight* books. Did they manage to recreate it in the films? Did they ever! Kristen Stewart and Robert Pattinson positively sizzle on screen. Catherine Hardwicke instantly saw a heated, unspoken connection – "What Rob and Kristen had is a multitude of feelings for each other. Complex feelings for each other. It was what we needed. Complex, intense fascination." The magnetism between the pair on screen has led to endless coverage of the young stars' real-life romance. What's the deal? Who cares, when there's another hot guy on the block! By the time *New Moon* was released, the Rob/Kristen mania was replaced with full-on Jacob fever! Taylor Lautner sent pulses racing with his new buff body, sexy eyes and laidback cool. Things really heated up in *Eclipse*, with Bella having to make a tough choice between two very worthy candidates – and Kristen relished acting out the love triangle. "I loved watching the three of them," she says. "There's literally a scene where Edward and Jacob, who are mortal enemies, are in a tent with a sleeping Bella in between them." Jealous, us?

Jacob & Edward

Beyond Twilight

Kristen has said how much she loved following Bella through four books, but what's next? The actress has been returning to her roots, working on more independent, arty films. Check her out in *The Runaways*, *K-11* (directed by her mum!), *The Yellow Handkerchief* and *An American Girl*.

"She's a unique girl. You really don't meet many people like Kristen."

Rob on his co-star

The A-Z of Kristen Stewart

This girl is pretty private, but we've dug up some cool facts on our favourite hipster . . .

A is for APPLE

Kristen can't get enough of her iPod.

B is for BLONDE

KStew's hair colour of choice before *Twilight*, although apparently, she prefers her darker look. And, of course, Edward prefers brunettes too!

C is for CONVERSE

Kristen made a bold style statement by matching a dressy frock with her trademark trainers at the 2009 MTV Movie Awards.

d is for DANCING

"Recently, I love forties Big Bands . . . and I started taking swing lessons," says Kris.

E is for EXERCISE

"I don't exercise," says Kristen. Lucky her!

F is for FASHION

As in, she's not into it! "I go outside, and I'm wearing a funky T-shirt and my hair is dirty, and people say, 'What's wrong with her? She needs to invest in a hairbrush.'"

G is for GUITAR

She plays really well and likes to jam with BFF Nikki Reed!

H is for HENRY MILLER

One of Kristen's favourite authors.

I is for ITALY

Kristen loved filming in Italy for *New Moon* and says, "there's nothing more exciting than discovering a new country."

K is for KNEES

Peter Facinelli says Kristen is naturally nervous: "I think she has that shaky knee syndrome and that's part of her charm."

J is for JOAN JETT

Kris played the '70s rock chick in *The Runaways* and the punk legend is now a close friend!

m is for MOWGLI

Kris just loves Disney movies, and *The Jungle Book* is her favourite.

L is for LED ZEPPELIN

Kristen loves her classic rock!

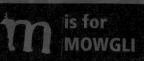

 is for NATALIE PORTMAN

The gorgeous actress makes KStew feel starstruck!

O is for OPERA

Soap opera, that is. Kristen says her life sometimes seems like "a ridiculous show . . . the Kristen show."

P is for PETS

KStew is the proud owner of dogs Oz, Jack and Lily, and a cat named Jella.

Q is for QUALIFICATIONS

Kristen acted out Bella's high-school graduation in *Eclipse*, but missed her own real-life ceremony due to filming. Luckily, she asked an extra to take a photo of her in costume, so she'd have her very own memento!

r is for ROBERT DE NIRO

Her favourite male actor.

S is for SMALL TALK

She hates it! "You can't expect anyone to get anywhere in ten minutes of a conversation."

T is for TEETH

Kristen says she has never had a Hollywood smile and used to get teased for her buck teeth!

U is for UNDERWEAR

The *Twilight* merchandise that most freaks her out is underwear adorned with Taylor's face!

V is for VEGEMITE

Kristen's Australian mum introduced her to the yummy spread, which is a bit like Marmite.

W is for WRITING

KStew loves expressing herself on paper: "I'm not a storyteller, but I love words; I love their effect."

X is for EX-BOYFRIEND

Kristen's break-up with long-term BF Michael Angarano fuelled those Robsten rumours . . .

y is for YEAH YEAH YEAHS

Kristen digs this cool New York band.

Z is for ZAC EFRON

Poor Zac and Vanessa Hudgens lost out to Kristen and RPattz for the Best Kiss trophy at the MTV Movie Awards, 2009. Even he had to admit, "They do have a great kiss."

Which Twilight Girl are You?

1. **You can wear your own clothes at school today! What do you pick?**

   a) The latest trend, maybe even something you customized yourself.
   b) Something flattering and sexy.
   c) The first thing you grab – probably jeans and a T-shirt.
   d) Something classic that you feel comfortable in.

2. **Which series of words best describes you?**

   a) Chatty, fun, sensitive.
   b) Gorgeous, quiet, protective.
   c) Shy, kind, clumsy.
   d) Caring, gentle, intelligent.

3. **What would you do in a spare afternoon?**

   a) Shop with the girls: fashion and fun!
   b) Take a long bath and paint your nails.
   c) Cosy up on the sofa and read a book.
   d) Make some delicious cookies for your friends.

4. **What kind of music do you like to listen to?**

   a) Pop or dance – anything you can jump around to!
   b) R'n'B – it's smooth and sexy.
   c) Rock or punk – you like music that's edgy and different.
   d) Classical – you like music that's beautiful and sensitive.

5. **What is your biggest flaw?**

   a) I tend to rush into things without thinking first.
   b) I get jealous and can sometimes be mean.
   c) I'm quite insecure and not sure if people really like me.
   d) I can worry too much about others and not enough about myself.

6. **How would you spend a perfect date with your guy?**

   a) Dancing and laughing the night away at a cool party.
   b) At a posh restaurant, both of you dressed up and feeling fabulous.
   c) On a long walk in the countryside, with a picnic, just for two.
   d) At home, eating a delicious meal you've cooked and chatting all night.

7. **What would your ideal home look like?**

   a) An open-plan loft apartment with lots of room for dinners and parties.
   b) A designer pad with all the mod cons and very stylish furniture.
   c) A pretty house in the countryside, somewhere peaceful.
   d) A beautifully decorated, large modern house, with family nearby.

8. **A boy is looking your way at a party. What do you do?**

   a) Go over and chat to him.
   b) Give him a sexy look back.
   c) Get embarrassed and look away.
   d) Smile in a friendly way.

9. **You're attending a big, flashy event. What do you wear?**

   a) A daring, stylish new dress in a deep purple, with unique silver jewellery.
   b) A sleek, bold red dress with a plunging neckline and killer heels.
   c) A pretty, powder-blue, chiffon tea dress . . . with trainers!
   d) A beautiful, classic, black dress with a simple necklace and a clutch bag.

10. **Which three qualities do you look for in a boyfriend?**

   a) Devoted, reserved, protective.
   b) Strong, brave, funny.
   c) Sensitive, intelligent, mysterious.
   d) Clever, calm, caring.

11. **Someone has said something nasty about you. What do you do?**

   a) Shrug it off – it shouldn't ruin your mood.
   b) Say bad things about them behind their back.
   c) Feel really upset, but don't tell anyone.
   d) Talk to your friends about it so you feel better.

Alice Cullen

Rosalie Hale

Esme Cullen

Bella Swan

Mostly As: *You're Alice Cullen*

You are vivacious, artistic and bursting with energy. While it may seem you live in your own unique little world, you are very open and love meeting new people. You are a wonderful friend and care deeply for those you love, and they adore you in return for your upbeat personality, amazing style and creativity.

Mostly Bs: *You're Rosalie Hale*

You are stunningly beautiful, aloof and very confident. People often misunderstand you and your quietness can come across as rude – but the truth is, it takes you a long time to trust anyone. Once you do let someone in, you are very passionate, loyal and protective of your loved ones.

Mostly Cs: *You're Bella Swan*

You are intelligent, kind and very brave. You are also very popular – although you don't always understand why, as you're not very confident. People love your sweetness and empathy, and you charm people without even trying! Deep down, you also have a hidden passion and intensity reserved for those close to you.

Mostly Ds: *You're Esme Cullen*

You are extremely caring, considerate and loving. People are instantly drawn to your warmth and compassion and you have some truly devoted friends. You have a very mature, clear perspective on things so you're great at giving advice. You love listening to and helping your loved ones.

BELLA SWAN
Beauty Guide

Bella is a fresh-faced, natural girl. Learn how to capture her subtle, delicate prettiness with our make-up tutorial and flutter those lashes in Biology class!

Start with your base. For a light, dewy finish, apply a tinted moisturiser to your face with your fingers, making sure to blend into the neck. Then, add a dusting of loose powder.

One

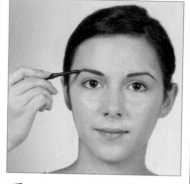

Two

Using an eyebrow pencil, finely fill in your brows. These shouldn't be too thick, but a subtle deepened brow intensifies the beauty of the eyes.

Three

Take a nude eyeshadow, one shade darker than your eyelids, and brush over the eye sockets.

Four

Apply a darker brown shadow into the crease, blending with a brush.

Using a soft brown kohl liner, smudge a fine line along the upper and lower lashes. Add a light slick of black mascara.

Five

Six

Rub a rose pink lipstick colour onto your lips to give them a slightly flushed look, and finish with a touch of lip balm for a kissable pout.

Don't forget Bella's pretty locks! She's a wash 'n' go girl, so you want to create a natural look. Use tongs to loosely curl a few pieces of hair and run some wax through the ends for a windswept finish. Has someone been hanging out at La Push beach?

TWILIGHTER
Isabelle, 14

Verdict:

"I love Bella's look! It is understated and easy to create, but still looks glamorous. Plus, all my friends loved the make-up and even commented on how similar I looked to the character."

KRISTEN STEWART
Beauty Guide

Kristen tends to keep things pretty low-key during the day, but transforms into a sultry, punky starlet by night. Follow our tutorial to recreate her striking look and channel your inner rebel!

For your base, choose a medium-coverage foundation and apply to your face and neck with a sponge or brush, blending until even. You want your face to look flawless.

One

Dab a liquid concealer onto blemishes and dot beneath your eyes to cover dark circles. Blend with a fine brush.

Two

Dust your face with a coating of loose powder to set it perfectly.

Fill in your brows with an eyebrow pencil to give a sharp and defined arc. You can also blend a dash of white eyeshadow under your brows to make them even more striking.

Three

Four

Apply a light grey eyeshadow over your entire eyelid with a brush, blending up towards your brows.

Seven

Define the eye with a black kohl liner. Draw a line close to the upper and lower lashes and smudge with a sponge brush. If you can manage it, draw a line all around your inner lids too – this will give a smoky effect.

Five

Brush a darker grey eyeshadow along the crease. Then, add a very dark grey or black shade at the outer corners of the eye and blend.

Six

. . . and Eight

Finish by applying a touch of pale pink lipstick to your mouth, and a dab of gloss.

To copy Kristen's cool, tousled hairstyle, use tongs to create loose curls all over your head, then separate roughly with your fingers, adding a touch of serum for glossy definition. Smoking hot!

TWILIGHTER
Charlotte, 19

Verdict:

"Kristen is gorgeous, but her look isn't something I would normally go for. However, the make-up made me feel very glamorous and sophisticated. My friends thought I looked great and I have since recreated the look many times myself."

Get the Look!

Need the finishing touch to complete your *Twilight* style transformation? Find out
how to look top-to-toe polished with this super-cool nail tutorial!

TWILIGHT NAILS

**These dark and lovely vamp-inspired nails
will give any outfit an edge!**

One

First, remove any old nail polish and shape
your nails with a file or emery board. File each nail tip
from corner to centre, and move the file in one
direction only – otherwise your nails will start to split.
An oval shape with a lightly squared-off tip
is the coolest way to go.

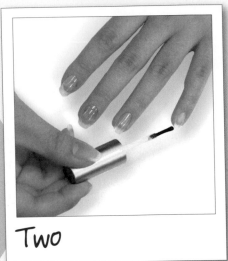

Two

Prepare your nails with a
clear base coat. This helps
stop polish chipping and
also means your nails
won't stain! Allow to dry
for a couple of minutes.

Three

Take a bottle of black nail polish and roll it gently between
your hands for about 30 seconds – this helps mix the
polish and stops bubbles forming. Now apply the first coat
to your nails. Paint a stripe in the middle of the nail, then
another to the left and right. Re-dip your brush into the
bottle each time you begin a new nail. Let your nails dry
completely for 5–10 minutes.

Four

Apply a second coat of
polish, so you get a rich,
intense colour. Again, let
your nails dry thoroughly
for 5-10 minutes.

Five

Now the fun really starts! We've used a red nail polish to give the effect of blood-tipped nails. Take a pillar-box red colour and carefully run the brush along the tips of the nails – you're not going for a neat French tip here, but an uneven drip effect, and every nail should look gorgeously unique!

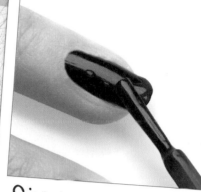

Six

Repeat the process on every nail, building up the red polish to get a really deep colour. For a final masterstroke, add some red drops on a couple of nails, too.

Seven

Finish by applying a clear topcoat. This seals and protects the colour and should keep your nails looking perfect for at least a week. Hot!

The Ultimate Fan Quiz

Do you know enough about Kristen to be her BFF?
Think you've got Robert and Taylor pegged?
You'd better have read this book from cover to
cover, cos it's time for the big test!

1. Which is Rob's favourite book in the *Twilight* series?
   a) *New Moon*
   b) *Eclipse*
   c) *Breaking Dawn*

2. How old was Taylor when he won the Karate Junior
   World Championship?
   a) 12
   b) 13
   c) 14

3. Where is Kristen's mum from?
   a) Argentina
   b) Armenia
   c) Australia

4. Who appeared on *The Nick & Jessica Variety Hour*
   early in their career?
   a) Robert
   b) Kristen
   c) Taylor

5. What was the name of Robert's old band?
   a) Bad Boys
   b) Bad Girls
   c) Bad Name

6. What is the name of Taylor's younger sister?
   a) Michaela
   b) Makena
   c) Marlene

7. Which star idolizes Robert De Niro?
   a) Kristen
   b) Robert
   c) Taylor

8. Which musical legend has Kristen played in a movie?
   a) Joan Baez
   b) Joan Jett
   c) Joni Mitchell

9. What is Patty's favourite scary movie?
   a) *The Shining*
   b) *The Omen*
   c) *The Exorcist*

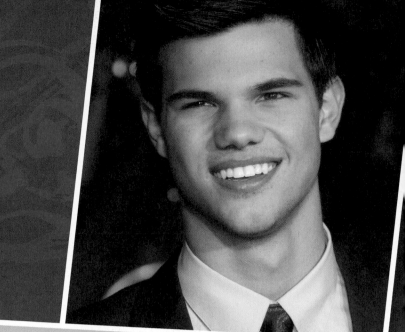

10. How many pounds of muscle weight did Tay pack on for *New Moon*?
    a) 30
    b) 20
    c) 40

11. Whose middle name is Thomas?
    a) Taylor
    b) Kristen
    c) Robert

12. What was the name of the movie in which Kristen took her first lead role?
    a) *Talk*
    b) *Listen*
    c) *Speak*

13. What star sign is RPattz?
    a) Gemini
    b) Aries
    c) Taurus

14. Which star does Taylor have the hots for?
    a) Britney Spears
    b) Megan Fox
    c) Scarlett Johansson

15. How many brothers does KStew have?
    a) 2
    b) 3
    c) 4

16. Which of the stars is the youngest?
    a) Taylor
    b) Kristen
    c) Robert

17. Who does Rob love to listen to?
    a) Van Halen
    b) Van Morrison
    c) Vanilla Ice

18. What was the name of Tay's first starring role?
    a) Sackboy
    b) Soulja Boy
    c) Sharkboy

19. Who was Kristen's director on *Into the Wild*?
    a) Steven Spielberg
    b) Sean Penn
    c) Spike Jonze

20. What did Rob's sisters call him as a kid?
    a) Claudia
    b) Christina
    c) Clara

21. Taylor shares his heritage with which Native American tribes?
    a) Opata and Pojoaque
    b) Odawa and Powhatan
    c) Ottawa and Potawatomi

22. Which star owns four pets?
    a) Robert
    b) Taylor
    c) Kristen

23. What is KStew's favourite Disney film?
    a) *The Jungle Book*
    b) *The Little Mermaid*
    c) *The Incredibles*

24. How tall is Rob?
    a) 6'0"
    b) 6'1"
    c) 6'2"

25. Which of these young starlets hasn't been linked with Taylor?
    a) Taylor Swift
    b) Vanessa Hudgens
    c) Selena Gomez

26. Who are Kristen's favourite rockers?
    a) Led Zeppelin
    b) Linkin Park
    c) Lynyrd Skynyrd

27. What brand of sunglasses does Rob favour?
    a) Prada
    b) D&G
    c) Ray-Ban

28. Where is Taylor from?
    a) Los Angeles
    b) Michigan
    c) Wisconsin

29. Which star likes to guzzle Diet Coke?
    a) Kristen
    b) Robert
    c) Taylor

30. Who is Kristen's favourite actress?
    a) Natalie Portman
    b) Nikki Reed
    c) Naomi Watts

Answers

Use the answers below to check how many
questions you got right. Give yourself two points
for every correct answer, add up your total
and find out how well you did!

1.	a	11.	c	21.	c
2.	a	12.	c	22.	c
3.	c	13.	c	23.	a
4.	c	14.	b	24.	b
5.	b	15.	b	25.	b
6.	b	16.	a	26.	a
7.	a	17.	b	27.	c
8.	b	18.	c	28.	b
9.	c	19.	b	29.	b
10.	a	20.	a	30.	a

How Well Do You Know the Stars?

0–20 points: New Fan

Not the greatest score! Perhaps you're new to Rob, Taylor and Kristen, or maybe you just need to try harder. See, if you want to join the Twilighters and call yourself an ultimate fan, you're going to have to do better than that. It's not that hard – all the answers are in this book. Now go back and read it again!

22–40 points: Firm Fan

You're not quite Robsessed, but you're on your way! You clearly have a solid knowledge of the star trio and can be happy with your not-quite-obsessive score. If you want to nudge your total up a notch, go back over the star profile pages with a fine-tooth comb.

42–50 points: Ultimate Fan

Wow. You really know your stuff! You've probably watched the *Twilight* films a million times, read everything you can about Rob, Taylor and Kristen, and wear a Team Edward or Team Jacob shirt under your clothes right? Well it's paid off. You can proudly call yourself a real fan of the stars and a true Twihard! Now go and gloat.

Pick a Team T-Shirt

Are you a Robsessive or a Taylor fanatic? Pick a side and make your very own Team Edward or Team Jacob T-shirt with our cool stencils!

What you will need:

- Clear sticky-backed plastic
- A black marker pen
- A craft knife
- A cutting mat or chopping board
- Some newspaper
- Some fabric paints
- A paintbrush
- A plain T-shirt
- A hot iron

Careful!
Make sure to ask an adult if you need help with the craft knife or iron.

1 Photocopy your chosen stencil from this book.

2 Lay a piece of unpeeled sticky-backed plastic over your copied image, shiny side up.

3 Trace the image beneath onto your plastic with a thin black marker pen.

4 Place the plastic onto a cutting mat or chopping board. Carefully cut out the image with a craft knife.

5 Cover a surface with newspaper and lay your T-shirt flat on top. Place a thick layer of newspaper inside your T-shirt too – you don't want the ink to leak through to the back!

6 Unpeel the backing from your plastic and stick the stencil to the T-shirt. If you don't get it right first time, you can peel it off and do it again!

Hot Tip!
Choose any colour T-shirt and paint that you like!

7 Using the paintbrush, dab your fabric paint onto the T-shirt, inside the stencil. Go right over the edges of your image. Leave it to dry overnight.

9 Place a sheet of plain paper over the print and iron over it to set the paint.

8 Carefully peel away the stencil to reveal your finished design.

Now wear it with pride!

Twispeak

Want to be a true Twihard? You've got to get the lingo right! Check out this dazzling dictionary.

Twilighter

A fan of Stephenie Meyer's *Twilight* Saga. Twilighters love the books, films and especially the actors and will be first in the queue on the opening night of *Breaking Dawn*.

Girl 1: Taylor Lautner is the hottest person to walk the planet.

Girl 2: You're a total Twilighter!

Twihard

An ultimate, obsessive fan of the *Twilight* series. Formed from the words 'Twilight' and 'die-hard', as in, 'die-hard fan'. A step up from a 'Twilighter', this person has an in-depth knowledge of the books and can get very upset if the movies change things up too much. They probably eat mushroom ravioli, quote the books a lot and tell everyone their last name is 'Cullen'.

Girl 1: Do you want some popcorn?

Twihard: You brought a snack?

Twituber

Twilighters and Twihards who also post *Twilight* tribute videos on YouTube.

Twituber: I just recreated a scene from *Eclipse* on my webcam!

Twilights

The bronze hair highlights RPattz sports in the movies. Twifans have been asking for these at salons!

Girl 1: Did you get your hair done?

Girl 2: Yep, I got Twilights.

OMJ

As above, but for the other team – 'Oh My Jacob!'

OMJ! Taylor's abs are so much better than Rob's!

Redward

A handy way to refer to both Robert Pattinson and Edward Cullen.

Girl 1: Do you like Rob or Edward better?

Girl 2: I can't choose. I like Redward.

Twiguy

A boy who is into the *Twilight* series. A pretty rare species.

I just saw a boy wearing a Forks baseball shirt. I think he's a Twiguy!

Robsessed

Displaying a complete and utter devotion to Robert Pattinson.

She's not just into RPattz, she's totally Robsessed.

OME

Stands for 'Oh My Edward!' As opposed to 'OMG!'

OME! The photos of RPattz in this book are so hot!

VIP

Very Important Prey. A human with supremely attractive blood, like Bella.

Edward would totally go for me, I'm VIP.

JACOB IS MY MAN!

I LOVE RPATTZ

I ♥ Twilight

MRS LAUTNER

PEACE. LOVE. TWILIGHT.

Bite Me!

PEACE. LOVE. TWILIGHT.

VAMPIRE MAGNET